MIKE PREPPER

Original edition

1st edition 2023

© 2023 by OsnaPlan-Verlag - Michael Gilsau

Eichenstraße 2, D-49143 Bissendorf

info@osnaplan.de

Editorial office: OsnaPlan-Verlag - Michael Gilsau

Cover design: https://de.fiverr.com/fashionerstudio

MIKE PREPPER

Home-Office 3.0 – Earn money online

Your path to more freedom and financial independence

Incl. bonus: C h a t G P T

Earn money online from home - easier than ever before!

Table of contents

IV. Earning opportunities through home work

V. Practical tips for successful work from home

VI. Conclusion and Outlook

I. Introduction

Why working from home is a good option

The world of employment has changed dramatically in recent years, and with the growing importance of the Internet and digitalization, new ways of working have emerged. One of them is working from home. Whether they are freelancers, self-employed or employees in a home office, more and more people are choosing to work from their own four walls.

But what makes working from home such an attractive option? Flexibility is one answer. Working from home allows you to be more creative with your work schedule and create your own work environment to suit your needs and requirements. You can choose where and when you work without having to settle for fixed hours or locations. This means more freedom and empowerment.

But working from home offers many more advantages. For example, you save time and money by not having to travel to work every day, and you can choose your own work clothes. You also usually have a better work-life balance, as you can better combine your work with your private life. This can have a positive impact on your health and well-being.

In this guide we will show you how to successfully earn money from home. We will introduce you to 20 different ways to find and successfully perform home-based work. We also give you practical tips and tricks on how to stay productive and organize your work in the best possible way. We are convinced that working from home is a great opportunity to achieve more freedom and financial independence.

The advantages of working from home

1. **Flexibility**

    Working from home gives you the flexibility to set your own hours and create your own schedule. You can balance your work with your personal life and decide when and where you want to work.

2. **Less stress**

    By working in your own home, you avoid the daily commute to work, which can lead to less stress and time pressure. You can focus on your work, feeling more relaxed and productive.

3. **Cost saving**

    Working from home not only saves you time, it saves you money. There are no transportation costs or expensive work clothes to pay, and you can take advantage of your own kitchen and refrigerator. One negative aspect that should be mentioned at this point is the issue of energy costs. As a rule, energy costs are higher because you are in your own home for a longer period of time.

4. **Better work-life balance**

    When you work from home, you can better take care of your family and friends, pursue your hobbies and interests, and better integrate your work into your life.

5. **Higher productivity**
    Working from home can help you be more productive and efficient. You can focus on your work without being interrupted by colleagues, phone calls or meetings.

6. **Increased autonomy**
    As a home-based worker, you have more control over your work and can tailor it to your needs and abilities. You can work more independently and make your own decisions.

7. **Better health**
    Working from home can also help you be healthier. You'll have more time for physical activity, healthy eating and relaxation. You can also avoid illnesses that can result from contact with other people in the office.

8. **More time for other interests**
    Since you no longer have a commute, you have more time for other interests and activities. You can make better use of your free time and spend more time with family and friends.

These are just a few of the benefits of working from home. There are many more, depending on your individual situation and personal preferences. However, this small selection clearly shows that working from home is very attractive and offers the following benefits.

II. Prerequisites and Preparations

The most important requirements for home work

1. **Discipline and motivation**
    Working from home requires discipline and motivation. You must be able to do your work without direct supervision and motivate yourself to be productive.

2. **Time Management Skills**
    Working from home requires good time management skills. You need to use your time effectively and create a realistic work schedule to ensure you get your work done on time.

3. **Suitable working environment**
    An appropriate work environment is important for working effectively from home. You will need a quiet, well-lit work area that is free of distractions so that you can work without interruption. If there are children in the home, you should set up times when the children will allow you to work undisturbed.

4. **Technical equipment**
    Working from home usually requires proper technical equipment such as computers, printers, scanners and telephones. You should make sure that you have the necessary equipment to do your work effectively.

5. **Reliable Internet Connection**

A reliable Internet connection is essential for working from home because you're likely to rely on online tools and resources. Ensure that you have a reliable Internet connection so that you can work online at all times.

6. **Skills and experience**

Depending on the type of work you want to do from home, you may need certain skills and experience. Make sure you have the necessary skills and knowledge to perform your job successfully.

7. **Support from family and friends**

Working from home can be lonely at times. It is important to have the support of your family and friends to support you in your work and motivate you when needed.

This list of requirements for working from home is not intended to be exhaustive, and of course you should always consider your own personal and individual situation. But if you take all of these factors into consideration, you will have a better chance of working from home successfully.

First preparations for a successful Home work

1. Consider what kind of work you want to do from home. There are many different ways to work from home. Consider which type of work best suits your skills, interests, and needs. It can be helpful to make a list and weigh the pros and cons of different options.

2. Explore your options. Once you have decided on the type of work you want to do, research the different ways you can do that type of work from home. There are many websites and resources that can help you research.

3. Create a work schedule. When working from home, it's important to create a realistic work schedule. Consider your work hours, breaks, and other obligations to ensure you have enough time to do your job effectively. Create an appropriate work environment. Make sure you have a suitable workspace that is well lit and free of distractions. You may want to set up an area that is separate from your work area if you have children.

4. Obtain the necessary equipment. Make sure you have the necessary work materials to do your job effectively. This may include a computer, a reliable internet connection, a phone, a printer, and other office supplies.

5. Set up a work routine. A regular work routine can help you stay productive and use your time more effectively. Consider setting fixed work hours and how you want to schedule your breaks.

6. Stay motivated! It is important to stay motivated when you are working from home. Consider what strategies can help you stay motivated, such as setting goals, establishing a reward system, or even dealing with any setbacks.

By preparing for your home-based business and following the steps above, you can have a better chance of working from home successfully. Keep in mind that working from home is not for everyone and there can be some challenges. However, it is a great option for people who value flexibility and autonomy at work.

III. Bonus: C h a t G P T
Earn money online from home –
easier than ever before!

What exactly is ChatGPT?

ChatGPT is a fascinating example of the progress of artificial intelligence. As a kind of "virtual assistant," ChatGPT can interact with people, answer questions, give advice, and even hold conversations.

ChatGPT is the result of years of research and development at OpenAI, one of the leading companies in the field of artificial intelligence. The idea behind the project was to create a system that is capable of communicating with humans in a natural way, while having human-like conversations.

The system is based on the GPT-4.0 architecture, a further development of the GPT-3.5 model from OpenAI. The abbreviation "GPT" stands for "Generative Pretrained Transformer". This is a type of neural network that is trained with a large amount of data. In this way, the model is able to react to a large number of inputs and generate corresponding outputs.

ChatGPT training is done by analyzing huge amounts of texts, such as books, articles, and online content. The model uses this data to recognize and understand patterns and relationships in speech. In this way, ChatGPT learns to have human-like conversations and respond to complex queries.

The system is capable of being used in many different areas. For example, ChatGPT can be used as a digital assistant in companies or as a support agent in customer service departments. The system can also be useful in education or healthcare to help pupils, students or patients.

Another advantage of ChatGPT is that it is constantly being developed. By training with new data and adapting the algorithms, the system can become better and better and be extended to a wide range of applications.

However, there are also critical voices that warn of the potential impact of ChatGPT and similar systems. For example, jobs in customer service or other areas could be replaced by automation. There is also a risk that the system will unintentionally reproduce prejudices or discrimination, as it is trained on the basis of existing data.

Overall, however, ChatGPT is a fascinating example of the progress of artificial intelligence and has the potential to change many areas of our lives.

The model can be used on different platforms and through different media. For example, it is possible to interact with ChatGPT via messaging apps or websites. Voice assistants such as Siri or Alexa also use similar technologies to communicate with users.

Working with ChatGPT

There are almost infinite possibilities how ChatGPT can be used in the profession for support. We would like to share some examples with you here.

1. **Content creation**
   ChatGPT can be used to create content for blogs, websites, social media platforms or online publications. You can sell the created content or use it for advertising revenue.

2. **Marketing and advertising campaigns**
   ChatGPT can help develop and optimize marketing and advertising campaigns for companies. You can work as a consultant for companies or create your own campaigns and sell them to companies.

3. **Text correction and optimization**
   ChatGPT can be used for text correction and SEO optimization. You can work here as a freelancer for companies or offer your own correction and optimization services.

4. **Chatbot Development**
   ChatGPT can be used to develop chatbots for businesses. You can work as a developer for companies or develop your own chatbots and sell them to companies.

5. **Translation services**

ChatGPT can be used to translate texts into different languages. You can work as a freelancer for companies or offer your own translation services.

6. **Data acquisition and analysis**

ChatGPT can be used to collect and analyze data in various industries. Here, you can work as a data analyst for companies or offer your own data analysis services.

7. **Chatbot dialog creation**

ChatGPT can help create and optimize dialogs for chatbots. You can work as a freelancer for companies or offer your own services for creating chatbot dialogs.

There are many ways ChatGPT can be used in the profession to earn money. However, it depends on the skills and knowledge of the individual what kind of services they can offer.

Applications in practice

Complementing the previously mentioned uses of ChatGPT, below are 10 specific examples of practical uses of ChatGPT.

1. **Customer Service**
    ChatGPT can be used in customer service to answer customer questions quickly and efficiently. This allows companies to provide customer service around the clock and respond to customer queries quickly.

2. **Education**
    ChatGPT can be used in education to support pupils and students. For example, questions about certain topics can be answered or ChatGPT can help with learning by giving feedback or providing information.

3. **Healthcare**
    ChatGPT can be used in healthcare to answer patient questions or provide medical information. This way, patients can be supported faster and more efficiently.

4. **Travel Management**
    ChatGPT can be used in travel management to answer questions about flight times, hotel bookings or itineraries. This way, travelers can be supported faster and more efficiently.

5. **Finance**

   ChatGPT can be used in the field of finance to answer questions about accounts, transfers or investment strategies. This way, customers can be supported quickly and efficiently.

6. **Human resources**

   ChatGPT can be used in human resources to answer employees' questions or provide information about working conditions and regulations.

7. **Entertainment**

   ChatGPT can also be used in the entertainment industry to interact with fans of celebrities or athletes or to offer games and quizzes.

8. **Marketing**

   ChatGPT can be used in marketing to answer customer questions or to provide information about products and services.

9. **E-Commerce**

   ChatGPT can be used in e-commerce to answer questions about orders, shipping or returning products. This way, customers can be supported quickly and efficiently.

10. **Public services**

    ChatGPT can be used in public services to answer questions about public transport, opening hours or public facilities. This way, users can be supported quickly and efficiently.

How can I use ChatGPT in practice?

To use ChatGPT successfully, follow these steps.

1. **Choose a suitable platform**
   ChatGPT is available on various platforms, including web apps, mobile apps or messaging platforms like WhatsApp or Facebook Messenger. Choose the platform that best suits your needs.

2. **Now formulate your questions or request**
   Think about what questions you want to ask ChatGPT. Try to formulate your questions clearly and precisely so that ChatGPT will understand them more easily. The more information you provide ChatGPT in your question, the better the result of the answer will be.

Practical examples:

Correctly formulated:

- "How can I increase my productivity in the home office?"
- "Can you give me a good recipe for gluten-free bread?"
- "What are the advantages and disadvantages of different CMS systems?"

<u>Incorrectly formulated:</u>

- "I need home office tips."
- "Give me a recipe for bread."
- "Tell me about CMS systems."

The incorrectly worded questions are too general and imprecise, which may confuse ChatGPT or cause it not to provide the information you want. The correctly worded questions, on the other hand, are clear and precise, which will help ChatGPT provide more accurate answers that can help you solve your problem or achieve your goals.

3. **Start the conversation**

    Open the selected chat platform and start the conversation with ChatGPT. In most cases, ChatGPT will automatically greet you and prompt you to ask your questions. For longer dialogs on the same topic, ChatGPT pays attention to the information already exchanged earlier in the conversation and continues to build on it.

4. **Give feedback**

    ChatGPT is designed to learn and improve from its experience. If you are satisfied with ChatGPT's response, you can give them feedback to show them that they are doing a good job. However, if you are not satisfied with the answer, give feedback as well so that ChatGPT can improve.

5. **Use the results**

    Once you have the information you need, you can use the results to solve your problems or achieve your goals. Use the information to make informed decisions or to improve your work or life.

6. **Stay polite**

    Although ChatGPT is a robot, it is important to remain polite and respectful. Avoid insulting ChatGPT or using it in the wrong way. Remember that ChatGPT is also used by others and is an important part of the online community.

By following these steps, you can successfully use ChatGPT and take advantage of its powerful artificial intelligence for your professional goals.

How do I create meaningful texts?

To create meaningful text with ChatGPT, it is essential to formulate and set the seed, context, and prompts correctly. Here is an explanation of how to use these elements correctly.

1. **Seed**

   The Seed is used by ChatGPT to start generating text. It is a short sequence of text that serves as a starting point for generating text. The seed should be a short but concise starting point that reflects the general direction of the text you want to write. For example, your seed could be "Artificial intelligence is one of the most exciting technologies of our time" if you want to write an article about AI.

2. **Context**

   Context refers to the information that ChatGPT should consider when generating text. The context can be anything that has an effect on the text generator, such as information about the topic, the target audience, the purpose of the text, and so on. To ensure that the generated text is consistent and relevant, it is important to clearly define the context.

3. **Prompts**

    Prompts are specific instructions or questions that are intended to cause ChatGPT to include certain information or topics in the text that is generated. Prompts can be very useful to guide text generation and ensure that the generated text meets the requirements. For example, a prompt might be "Describe the benefits of AI for businesses" or "Explain how a neural network works".

You can effectively control ChatGPT's text generation and generate meaningful text that meets requirements and expectations by using Seed, Context and Prompts wisely.

How can ChatGPT organize and structure a text in an appealing way?

By responding to specific guidance and input, ChatGPT can help you structure a text and create an attractive outline. Here are some steps you can follow to have ChatGPT create a structured outline for you.

1. Define the topic and purpose of the text you want to write. Think about the main points you want to cover and the subtopics or details you want to include in the text.

2. Use specific instructions "Prompts" to give an overview of the topic of the text. State a clear question or topic on which you want to write.

3. Use "Seed" and "Context" to steer the model in a specific direction and ensure that the text is tailored to the desired topic. For example, you can specify keywords, key phrases, or some key points to be covered in the text.

4. After you have made the input, ChatGPT will generate a response. Review the generated texts and select the parts you want to include in your outline. Arrange the text fragments in a logical order and write a short summary for each section.

5. Use the information you got from the generated text to write your own summary and introduction. Make sure the outline is well-structured and logical, with a clear hierarchy of main points and subtopics.

6. Review your outline and text carefully to make sure they are clear, understandable, and serve the purpose of the text.

Overall, when it comes to structuring a text and creating an appealing outline, ChatGPT can be a valuable resource. With the right input and guidance, ChatGPT can help you organize your ideas and speed up the writing process.

Use ChatGPT as a coach for your own work

ChatGPT can be used as a coach for your own work in several ways.

1. **Feedback on written texts**
    You can use ChatGPT to get feedback on your written texts. Give ChatGPT a sample of your text and let it suggest a revision. Read the revised text and feedback carefully and use it to improve your own text.

2. **Generating ideas**
    If you are having trouble generating new ideas for a project or task, you can use ChatGPT to generate ideas. Give ChatGPT a topic or question and let it generate a list of ideas. Use these ideas as a starting point for your own thinking and creative processes.

3. **Questions and answers**
    ChatGPT can also be used as a coach for questions and answers. If you are having trouble finding an answer to a particular question, type the question into ChatGPT and let it generate an answer. Review the answer carefully and use it to support your own thinking and research.

4. **Source of inspiration**
    ChatGPT can also be used as a source of inspiration. Let ChatGPT generate a random text and read through it. Use the ideas or phrases you like to improve or develop your own projects or tasks.

It is important to note that ChatGPT is a tool and cannot replace all aspects of a human coaching relationship. Use ChatGPT as a complement to your own work and combine it with human feedback and coaching to get the best results.

Are there any restrictions on the use of ChatGPT?

Yes, there are some restrictions on the use of ChatGPT that should be taken into account.

1. **Limited knowledge**
    Although ChatGPT is capable of performing a variety of tasks, its answers are based only on the data it was able to access during its training. Thus, if a user asks a question that is outside the scope of ChatGPT's training data set, ChatGPT may not be able to provide an appropriate answer.

2. **Data Quality**
    The quality of the data on which ChatGPT is trained can affect its ability to provide appropriate responses. If the training data is insufficient or inaccurate, this can lead to poor results.

3. **Abuse**
    As with any other technology, ChatGPT can be misused. For example, it can be used to spread disinformation or fake news, or to use inappropriate or offensive language.

4. **Privacy Policy**
    Because ChatGPT accesses data and information that users provide, there is a possibility that users' privacy may be violated. It is important to ensure that the platforms on which ChatGPT is used implement sufficient security measures to protect user privacy.

5. **Bias**

   Through the training dataset on which it is based, ChatGPT may inherit unconscious biases. For example, if the dataset has a bias towards a particular group or culture, this may influence ChatGPT's responses. It is important to ensure that the training dataset is balanced and free of bias. This will ensure that ChatGPT responds appropriately and fairly.

Glossary and explanation of common terms in the field of artificial intelligence

Artificial Intelligence (AI)

Artificial intelligence refers to machines that are capable of performing human-like intelligence tasks, such as speech recognition, image recognition, word processing, and decision making.

Machine Learning

Machine learning is a method of AI that uses algorithms to learn from data and make predictions without being explicitly programmed.

Deep Learning

Deep learning is an advanced form of machine learning that uses layered neural networks to perform complex tasks like image recognition and language processing.

Neural network

A neural network is an algorithm inspired by the way the human brain works and consists of many interconnected neurons.

Natural Language Processing (NLP)

Natural language processing refers to the process of processing human speech by computers, including speech recognition and speech generation.

Computer Vision

Computer vision refers to the process of processing images and video by computers, including image recognition and object detection.

Reinforcement Learning

Reinforcement learning is a method of machine learning in which an algorithm can learn through trial-and-error by being rewarded for good decisions and punished for bad ones.

Big Data

Big Data refers to large data sets that are too large or too complex to be processed using traditional data processing methods.

Algorithm

An algorithm is a step-by-step guide for solving a problem or performing a task by a computer.

IoT (Internet of Things)

The Internet of Things refers to the networking of physical devices such as sensors, cameras and home appliances to collect and share data.

IV. Earning opportunities through home work

1. Online surveys

A popular way to make money from home is through online surveys. Businesses and organizations often need feedback from consumers to improve their products and services and optimize their marketing strategies. In order to earn money or coupons, you can sign up with survey sites and take surveys on a regular basis.

You need to sign up with reputable survey sites to earn money from online surveys. Toluna, Swagbucks and GlobalTestMarket are some popular sites. You can fill out your profiles on these sites to ensure that you only receive surveys that match your profile.

Depending on the site and survey, payment for online surveys varies. Some surveys may only take a few minutes and earn you a few cents. Other surveys may take longer and earn you several dollars. To maximize your income, it's important to take surveys regularly.

Although online surveys are an easy way to earn money from home, you should be aware that there are some drawbacks. The pay can be relatively low, and it can be difficult to find enough surveys to earn a steady income.

Also, there are many fraudulent websites that promise to offer high payments for surveys, but are actually just out to collect your personal information. Make sure that you use reputable survey websites and read the terms of use carefully before signing up to their sites.

Useful web links on the topic of online surveys:

- Toluna – https://de.toluna.com

- Swagbucks – https://www.swagbucks.com

- GlobalTestMarket – https://www.globaltestmarket.com

- LifePoints – https://www.lifepointspanel.com

- Meinungsplatz – https://www.meinungsplatz.de

- EntscheiderClub – https://www.entscheiderclub.de

- Meinungsstudie – https://www.meinungsstudie.de

- Ipsos i-Say – https://www.ipsos.com/de-de

- GfK Panel – https://www.gfk.com/de

2. Virtual assistant activities

As a VA, you can provide administrative, organizational, and technical support to businesses and individuals while working out of your home. As a VA, you can perform tasks such as managing email, data entry, scheduling travel, managing social media, accounting, customer service, and more.

There are many online platforms to find VA jobs, including Upwork, Fiverr, and Remote.co. Of course, you can also apply directly to companies or individuals who are in need of VA services and offer your services.

You should have administrative, organizational, and technical skills to be successful as a VA. Since you will be interacting with clients and colleagues, you should be able to organize and prioritize your work effectively and have excellent communication skills.

Compensation for VA jobs is dependent on the nature and complexity of the job. Some jobs may be paid on an hourly basis, while others may have a flat fee. It's important to have clear agreements with your clients. Make sure you're getting paid appropriately for your work.

Virtual assistant jobs are particularly suitable for people with good administrative skills and experience, and offer a flexible way to earn money from home.

Useful web links to find jobs as a virtual assistant (VA):

- Upwork – https://www.upwork.com

- Fiverr – https://www.fiverr.com

- FlexJobs – https://www.flexjobs.com

- Guru – https://www.guru.com

- PeoplePerHour – https://www.peopleperhour.com

- Indeed –
  https://www.indeed.com/q-Virtual-Assistant-jobs.html

- Remote.co –
  https://remote.co/remote-jobs/virtual-assistant

- Virtual Assistant Jobs –
  https://www.virtualassistantjobs.com

- Freelancer –
  https://www.freelancer.com/jobs/virtual-assistant

3. Web design and development

You are responsible for designing, creating, and programming websites and applications as a web designer and developer. You can either freelance or work for a web design or marketing agency. The advantage of freelancing is that you can work from home. This gives you more flexibility.

You need to be skilled in user interface design and programming in various languages such as HTML, CSS, JavaScript, PHP and more to be successful as a web designer and developer. You will also need to be experienced in using Content Management Systems like WordPress, Magento or Shopware.

In addition, you should be able to design websites that are in tune with the needs of your clients. This includes keeping up with the latest design trends and technological developments.

You can take online courses, webinars, or tutorials to improve your skills as a web designer and developer. There are many platforms such as Udemy, Lynda, or Skillshare that offer courses on various topics such as web design, web development, or user experience.

You can also find jobs on platforms like Upwork, Freelancer, or Fiverr. Another option is to market your services directly to customers by creating your own website and supplementing it with advertising on social media sites such as Facebook and Instagram.

Web design and development projects can be paid on a flat rate basis or by the hour. Compensation depends on the type and scope of the project, as well as your experience and skills.

Overall, working as a web designer and developer is a great way to work from home and use your skills in a fast-paced and exciting industry. However, it requires a lot of attention and dedication to be successful and keep clients happy.

Useful web links that can help you learn more about web design and development and deepen your knowledge:

- **Codecademy** – https://www.codecademy.com
  An interactive online learning platform that offers free courses in HTML, CSS, JavaScript and other programming languages.

- **Udemy** – https://www.udemy.com
  An online platform for e-learning courses where you can find a variety of courses on web design, web development and other topics.

- **W3Schools** – https://www.w3schools.com
  A free online web development resource that provides tutorials and reference material on HTML, CSS, JavaScript, and other web technologies.

- **CSS-Tricks** – https://css-tricks.com
  A website with tutorials, code snippets and resources on CSS.

- **A List Apart** – https://alistapart.com
  An online platform offering articles and tutorials on web design and development.

- **SitePoint** – https://www.sitepoint.com
  An online platform for web developers and designers with articles, tutorials and courses on various topics related to web development.

- **Smashing Magazine** – https://www.smashingmagazine.com
  An online magazine for web designers and developers that features articles and tutorials on various topics such as UX design, web development and front-end techniques.

4. Copywriting and Content Creation

Copywriting and content creation are other ways to make money from home. If you enjoy writing and have a creative streak, you can use your talent to create copy and content for businesses and websites.

Here are steps you can take to prepare for a career in copywriting and content creation.

- **Improve your writing skills**
  If you want to become a good writer, you should improve your writing skills. Read books, articles, and blogs to familiarize yourself with different writing styles and techniques.

- **Choose your niche**
  There are many types of content you can create, from blog posts to social media posts to product descriptions and e-books. Think about what type of content you can best create and what topic interests you.

- **Create a portfolio website**
  To convince potential clients, you should create a portfolio website where you can showcase your best work. Here you can also include your contact information and pricing information.

- **Network**

  Use social media and professional networks like LinkedIn to connect with other writers and potential clients. You can also participate in online forums and writing groups to get feedback and support.

- **Work on your marketing**

  To attract clients, you need to market your services. Create a marketing kit with a price list and examples of your work and send it to potential clients.

More tips for successful copywriting and content creation:

- Write clear and concise copy that speaks to the needs of your target audience.

- Pay attention to spelling and grammar.

- Adhere to the client's specifications regarding the style and tone of the texts.

- Stay up to date on content trends and best practices.

There are many websites such as Textbroker, Content.de or even Upwork where you can find jobs as a copywriter or content creator. If you specialize in a particular niche, you can also search for companies that need content in that niche.

Useful web links that can help you find jobs as a copywriter or content creator:

- Textbroker – https://www.textbroker.de

- Content.de – https://www.content.de

- Upwork – https://www.upwork.com

- Fiverr – https://www.fiverr.com

- Freelancer – https://www.freelancer.de

- ClearVoice – https://www.clearvoice.com

- Constant Content – https://www.constant-content.com

There are also some online courses and resources that can help you improve your writing skills and succeed in the world of content marketing:

- Copyblogger – https://copyblogger.com

- Hubspot Academy – https://academy.hubspot.com

- Udemy – https://www.udemy.com

- Coursera – https://www.coursera.org

- Skillshare – https://www.skillshare.com

With these resources, you can improve your skills and make a good name for yourself in the copywriting and content creation market in the long run.

5. Translation and editing

A high level of fluency in at least two languages is required to work as a home translator or proofreader. As a general rule, to work as a translator or proofreader, you should be fluent in one of the foreign languages and have a perfect command of your native language.

Good knowledge of grammar, spelling, syntax, and punctuation is important. If you work as a translator, you should also be able to translate the style, nuance and meaning of the original text into the target language.

Another important factor is that, as a translator or proofreader, you need to be reliable and deliver the work to your clients on time. Meeting deadlines is essential to earning the trust of your clients and building a good reputation.

To work successfully as a home translator or proofreader, you can take specialized courses or certificates to improve your language skills and prove your abilities. You can also find jobs that match your skills and experience on many online job boards and platforms.

Establishing yourself in the marketplace and building a good reputation is an important part of being a successful work-from-home translator or proofreader.

This can be achieved through high quality work, good time management and communication with your customers.

Useful web links that can help you find jobs as a translator or proofreader:

- **ProZ.com** – https://www.proz.com
  One of the largest online job boards for translators and interpreters. Here you can search for jobs, present your profile and participate in discussions.

- **Upwork** – https://www.upwork.com
  An online platform where freelancers can find jobs in various fields, including translation and editing.

- **Freelancer.com** – https://www.freelancer.com
  A similar platform to Upwork where you can find jobs in various fields, including translation and editing.

- **TextMaster** – https://www.textmaster.com
  An online translation, editing and content creation platform aimed at businesses.

- **TranslatorsCafé** –
  https://www.translatorscafe.com
  Another popular job board for translators, offering jobs in various languages and subject areas.

6. Social Media Management

Another popular alternative to make money from home is social media management. Essentially, this refers to managing a company's or individual's social media presence. This includes content creation, post scheduling, comment management, and social media channel performance analysis.

Depending on the client, the requirements for social media management jobs can vary greatly. Some possible requirements may include:

- Proficiency in various social media platforms including Facebook, Twitter, Instagram, TikTok and LinkedIn.

- Ability to create engaging and creative content

- Experience in creating social media strategies

- Understanding of social media analytics tools to measure the success of campaigns

- Customer focus and ability to communicate effectively with clients or customers

Social media management can be a lucrative business, as many companies have realized how important a strong social media presence is to their success. If you have the necessary skills, you can search for social media management jobs through online job boards or social media groups.

Useful web links that can help you search for social media management jobs:

- Upwork – https://www.upwork.com

- Freelancer – https://www.freelancer.com

- Indeed – https://www.indeed.com

- Glassdoor – https://www.glassdoor.com

- LinkedIn Jobs – https://www.linkedin.com/jobs

It can also be helpful to search relevant social media groups or forums and ask about jobs or opportunities.

7. E-commerce and online sales

Another great way to make money from home is through e-commerce and online sales. There are many opportunities to sell products online and run your own online store with the increasing popularity of online shopping, especially after the Corona Pandemic.

There are several platforms that make it relatively easy to create your own online store if you are interested in doing so. These include sites like Shopify, Wix, and Squarespace. These platforms offer templates and tools for creating professional-looking websites and selling products online.

Alternatively, you can sell products on online marketplaces like Amazon, eBay, Yatego, or Etsy. These platforms allow you to sell your products to a wider audience and have systems in place to process orders and payments. As your online business grows and your sales increase, you may also want to consider purchase processing software to help you manage your business more professionally. There are providers such as JTL or Dreamrobot.

If you don't want to sell your own products, you can also work as an affiliate marketer and promote other companies' products. You earn a commission when someone buys a product based on your recommendation.

To be successful in e-commerce, you need knowledge in the following areas:

- Product photography and description

- Knowledge of SEO (Search Engine Optimization) and online marketing

- Experience in customer service and communication

- Knowledge of managing online payments and shipping

- Basic legal knowledge would be an advantage

There are many online resources that can help you set up an online store or sell products in online marketplaces. Some popular websites are:

- Amazon Seller Central – https://sellercentral.amazon.de

- eBay Seller Center – https://www.ebay.de/help/selling

- Etsy Seller Handbook – https://www.etsy.com/seller-handbook

- Shopify – https://www.shopify.de

- Yatego – https://merchants.yatego.com

With a little time and effort, you can grow your online store into a successful and lucrative business.

Here is a small selection of the largest marketplaces where you can start your online business:

1.   Shopify – https://www.shopify.de

2.   Magento – https://magento.com

3.   Etsy – https://www.etsy.com/de

4.   eBay – https://www.ebay.de

5.   WooCommerce – https://woocommerce.com

6.   Yatego – https://merchants.yatego.com

7.   Zalando Marketplace – https://marketplace.zalando.de

8.   Otto Marketplace – https://www.otto-marketplace.de

9.   Amazon Marketplace – https://services.amazon.de/programme/verkaufen.html

8. Affiliate marketing

Affiliate Marketing is a way to make money online by promoting other companies' products or services and earning commissions for each successful sale or lead generated.

There are three important parties in affiliate marketing: the merchant (also called the advertiser), the publisher (also called the affiliate), and the customer. The merchant provides the product or service, the publisher promotes the product or service, and the customer is the one who will ultimately purchase or use the product or service.

A publisher can promote a merchant's products or services in several ways. One way is to place an affiliate link or banner on your website. When a customer clicks on the link or banner and purchases the product or service or takes a specific action, the publisher receives a commission.

Another option is e-mail marketing. The publisher can build an email list and send emails to its subscribers to promote the merchant's products or services. When a customer purchases products or takes a specific action based on these emails, the publisher receives a commission.

One of the biggest advantages of affiliate marketing is that it eliminates the need for you to develop your own product or service, allowing you to simply promote the products or services of other companies in exchange for compensation for successful sales or lead generation.

There are a variety of affiliate networks that connect publishers with merchants and handle the processing of commissions.

It is important to find a niche that you understand and where you have a loyal audience in order to be successful in affiliate marketing. It is also important to choose products or services that fit this niche and are of high quality. The publisher should also make sure that he or she has enough traffic on his or her website or email list to generate enough clicks on his or her affiliate links or banners.

Overall, affiliate marketing can be a lucrative way to make money online. If you find the right niche and focus on high quality products or services. However, it also requires a certain amount of work and patience to be successful.

Useful web links about affiliate marketing:

- **AWIN** – https://www.awin.com/de
  A well-known affiliate network that brings together companies and publishers to do affiliate marketing together.

- **Digistore24** – https://www.digistore24.com
  A platform that allows online entrepreneurs to sell their products through affiliate marketing.

- **Affilorama** – https://www.affilorama.com
  A comprehensive learning platform that teaches you everything you need to know about affiliate marketing. It offers both free and paid resources and tools.

- **Affiliate-Marketing.de** –
  https://www.affiliate-marketing.de
  Here you will find a lot of information about affiliate marketing including tips & tricks as well as current trends.

- **Affiliate Summit** –
  https://www.affiliatesummit.com
  A premier conference and networking event for affiliate marketing professionals. A wealth of resources and information is available here.

9. Creative writing and book authorship

Creative writing and book authorship are also great ways to make money from home. If you love to write and have a passion for literature, this activity can help you realize your dream of a career as a writer and earn money at the same time.

You can work from home and create your own stories, novels, poems and other literary works as a creative writer or book author. You can self-publish your work or have it published by a publisher to bring it to a wider audience. There are many ways to market your work, including social media, readings and signings, and writing contests.

Writing and practicing regularly, as well as editing and refining your work to ensure it is of high quality, is important to being a successful book author. It can also be helpful to find a community of like-minded people to provide support and feedback.

There are other ways to use your writing skills to make money from home. These include ghostwriting, editing, and proofreading. As a ghostwriter, you can write for others who may not have the time or talent to write themselves.

Editing and proofreading are also important services for writers, as they can help to ensure that your work is free of errors and that it is well written.

It can be very interesting and exciting to make money from home as a creative writer or book author. However, it also takes a lot of dedication and practice to be successful.

Useful web links on creative writing and book authorship:

- Autorenwelt – https://www.autorenwelt.de

- Schreibnacht – https://www.schreibnacht.de

- BoD – Books on Demand – https://www.bod.de

- Autorenforum – https://www.autorenforum.de

- Schreibwerkstatt – https://www.schreibwerkstatt.co.at

- Selfpublisherbibel – https://www.selfpublisherbibel.de

- Verband deutscher Schriftstellerinnen und Schriftsteller – https://kunst-kultur.verdi.de/literatur/vs

10. Podcasting and YouTube

Podcasts and YouTube videos are things you've probably heard of. They're popular media formats. They're often used for entertainment or information. But podcasts and YouTube can also be used to make money from home.

Podcasts are recorded audio or video that can be accessed online. These recordings can be created on various topics such as politics, sports, lifestyle or business. There are many successful podcasts that have a large audience, which makes them attractive to advertisers. So, if you have a passion for a certain topic and enjoy speaking or doing interviews, podcasting could be an interesting alternative for you.

YouTube offers similar opportunities to podcasting, but in the form of video content. There are countless YouTubers who are very successful and have millions of subscribers. These are often beauty, gaming, comedy or tutorial videos on specific topics. Again, advertising is an important source of income for YouTubers. So YouTube could be an exciting option for you if you enjoy being in front of the camera, have creative ideas and some talent in video production.

To be successful in this field, it is important to build a loyal following.This means: You must continually create high-quality content that engages your audience. It's also important to find a clear niche and specialize in a specific topic to appeal to a target audience.

With podcasting and YouTube, there are many different ways to make money. Advertising is one of the most popular ways to make money. If you have a lot of viewers or listeners, advertisers may take notice and pay you to place their ads in your videos. Sponsorship is also an option, where you get paid to mention or feature a particular product or brand. You can also offer your own products or services related to your topic, such as merchandise or online courses.

Podcasting and YouTube offer many opportunities for creative people to make money. However, it also takes a lot of creativity and dedication to be successful. However, this could be the perfect way for you to make money from home if you have a passion for sharing a particular topic and some talent for audio or video production.

Overview of some well-known YouTubers in the field of podcasting and video production:

- Gronkh –
  https://www.youtube.com/user/Gronkh

- Julienco –
  https://www.youtube.com/user/juliencotv

- LeFloid –
  https://www.youtube.com/user/LeFloid

- Julia Beautx –
  https://www.youtube.com/JuliaBeautx

- Marc Friedrich –
  https://www.youtube.com/MarcFriedrich7

- Game Two –
  https://www.youtube.com/c/GameTwo

- MrWissen2go –
  https://www.youtube.com/c/MrWissen2go

- Moin Yamina –
  https://www.youtube.com/c/MoinYamina

- Die Filmfabrik –
  https://www.youtube.com/c/DieFilmfabrik

- Florian Homm –
  https://www.youtube.com/FlorianHommOfficial

- Rocket Beans TV –
  https://www.youtube.com/c/RocketBeansTV

The channels mentioned here cover a wide range of topics, including gaming, science, finance, education, culture, true crime, comedy, and much more. There are countless active YouTubers these days, so let the diversity of what's on offer inspire you for your own projects.

11. Online coach and consultant

As an online coach or consultant, you have the opportunity to offer your expertise or experience in a specific area to other people and help them achieve their goals. You can offer your coaching or consulting through various platforms such as Skype, Zoom or similar tools, allowing you to work from the comfort of your home.

To be successful as an online coach or consultant, you should have expertise and experience in your field, as well as a good understanding of your clients' needs. Good time management and effective communication skills are also critical to your success as an online coach or consultant.

Possible industries for online coaching or consulting:

- Career counseling

- Personality development

- Financial planning and consulting

- Fitness and health

- Relationship counseling

There are numerous platforms and websites where you can offer your coaching or consulting services, such as Coach.me, BetterHelp, or Clarity.fm.

It is also possible to offer your services on your own website and promote them through targeted marketing.

As an online coach or consultant, you can offer your services on an hourly or flat rate basis. The price often depends on your expertise and experience, as well as the demand in your specific area.

Useful web links about online coaching and counseling:

- Coach.me – https://www.coach.me

- BetterHelp – https://www.betterhelp.com

- Clarity.fm – https://clarity.fm

- Coachy – https://www.coachy.net

- CoachHub – https://www.coachhub.io

- Talkspace – https://www.talkspace.com

- 7Mind – https://7mind.de

- Headspace – https://www.headspace.com

- Calm – https://www.calm.com

- Lifesum – https://www.lifesum.com

- Noom – https://www.noom.com

12. Photography and graphic design

It is becoming increasingly popular to earn money as a photographer or graphic designer from home. Businesses and individuals are increasingly looking for professional photos and graphics to enhance their online presence as social media and online marketing become more important.

As a work-from-home photographer, you can produce stock photos for stock photo agencies or accept commissions from clients who are in need of portraits, wedding photos or product shots. To be successful in this field, you will need good equipment as well as knowledge of image editing.

As a homebased graphic designer, you'll have the opportunity to take on a variety of tasks. These include creating logos, flyers, brochures, banners, and more. Knowledge of graphic design tools such as Adobe Photoshop, Illustrator or InDesign is a plus. Creativity and an eye for aesthetics are also a plus.

Both of these options offer a high degree of flexibility and the ability to work from home and to bring your own projects to life. However, it is important to have a good knowledge of how to market your own work and to have a network of contacts in order to reach potential clients.

Also, with so many people offering their services, there is a lot of competition in these areas. To stand out from the competition, it is advisable to focus on a specific niche market and specialize in a particular area.

Overall, a really interesting way to be creative and make money at the same time is through home-based photography and graphic design opportunities. This could be the way to go if you have a passion for visual aesthetics and enjoy expressing yourself creatively.

Useful web links about photography and graphic design:

- **Canva** – https://www.canva.com
  Canva is an online design platform that allows users to create graphics, flyers, posters, cards and other designs.

- **Shutterstock** – https://www.shutterstock.com/de
  Shutterstock is a platform where users can buy and sell royalty-free images and videos.

- **Photoshop** –
  https://www.adobe.de/products/photoshop.html
  Photoshop is an image editing program from Adobe used by professional photographers and graphic designers.

- **iStockphoto** – https://www.istockphoto.com/de
  iStockphoto is another platform where users can buy and sell royalty-free images and videos.

- **Fotolia** – https://www.fotolia.com
  Also at Fotolia the user can buy and sell royalty-free images and videos.

There are also many online courses and tutorials that teach users how to improve their photography and design skills.

Some examples of these are:

- **CreativeLive** – https://www.creativelive.com
  CreativeLive offers live and on-demand courses on a variety of topics including photography and design.

- **Udemy** –
  https://www.udemy.com/topic/fotografie
  Udemy is an online learning platform where users can find courses on various topics such as photography and design.

- **Skillshare** –
  https://www.skillshare.com/browse/photography
  Skillshare is an online learning platform where users can find courses on various topics related to photography and design.

13. App development and programming

Another option for a successful home business is app development and programming. With the increasing popularity of smartphones and tablets, the demand for apps for various purposes is also growing.

You usually need a good knowledge of programming languages like Java, Swift, PHP or Python to become an app developer or programmer. However, there are also tools like App Builder that allow you to create simple apps without having to know how to code.

From developing mobile games to creating productivity apps to programming advanced web applications, working as an app developer can be very diverse.

Looking for project work on freelance platforms like Upwork, Freelancer.de or Fiverr is one way to work from home as an app developer. Here, developers can search for jobs that match their skills and interests and communicate with clients to clarify their requirements and complete their work.

Creating your own apps and selling them on the App Store or Google Play Store is another way to work as a home-based app developer. However, this requires not only programming skills, but also knowledge of marketing and sales.

An important factor for success as an app developer is the ability to constantly develop and keep up with the latest technologies and trends in the industry. This also includes the willingness to train oneself and regularly attend trainings and courses.

In summary, working as an app developer is a challenging and lucrative opportunity, but one that requires in-depth knowledge of programming and technology, as well as certain business skills.

Useful web links about app development and programming:

- Codecademy – https://www.codecademy.com

- Udacity – https://www.udacity.com

- Coursera – https://www.coursera.org

- edX – https://www.edx.org

- GitHub – https://github.com

- Apple Developer – https://developer.apple.com

- Android Developers – https://developer.android.com

- Microsoft Developer – https://developer.microsoft.com

On the aforementioned sites, you'll find a wealth of information, resources, and tools for aspiring app developers and programmers. Apple Developer, Android Developers, and Microsoft Developer are official developer platforms where you can find the tools and documentation you need to develop apps for their respective platforms.

Codecademy, Udacity, Coursera, and edX offer online courses that teach the basics of programming and app development, helping you gain the skills and knowledge you need. These courses range from beginner courses to advanced topics like machine learning and artificial intelligence.

GitHub is a web-based version control system used by developers to manage and share their projects. It's an important part of the development process and a great resource for collaborating with other developers.

14. Online market research

Online market research is the collection and analysis of data to support marketing decisions. Online research can take a variety of forms, including surveys, focus groups, and observational studies. Companies hire research firms to collect data to help them improve their products and services or develop new products and services.

Survey participants in an online research study may be paid for answering various questions or participating in focus groups or observational studies. Payment is often based on how much time and effort the participant puts into the study. There are also some sites that allow users to earn points that can be redeemed for cash or gift cards by completing online surveys or participating in other types of research activities.

If you want to participate in online market research, there are many reputable websites and market research companies that offer such opportunities. However, you should be careful when choosing a website because there are many scams where people promise to earn a lot of money but in the end they do not get paid at all.

It is important to read the terms and conditions and other users' reviews before signing up for an online market research website.

Overall, participating in online market research can be an easy and flexible way to earn money from home. It does not require any special skills or experience, just your own opinion and some time.

Useful web links on the topic of online market research:

- Respondent – https://www.respondent.io

- UserTesting – https://www.usertesting.com

- Toluna – https://www.toluna.com

- Swagbucks – https://www.swagbucks.com

- Vindale Research – https://www.vindale.com

- Ipsos – https://www.ipsos.com/de-de

- YouGov –
https://today.yougov.com/join-community

- Google Opinion Rewards –
https://surveys.google.com/google-opinion-rewards

15. Data Entry and Data Acquisition

Data entry and data capture are critical activities for businesses, organizations, and other entities. They involve the collection, verification, and manipulation of data in electronic form. Data entry often involves simpler tasks such as transcribing information, while data capture involves more complex processes that involve merging and preparing data from multiple sources.

Data entry and data capture activities may include, for example, entering addresses, verifying records for accuracy, entering data into databases, and merging data from different sources. It is an activity often used to conduct surveys, market research, and customer interviews.

It can often make sense for companies to outsource these tasks to save time and resources. This allows employees to focus on the company's core business while data processing is outsourced.

The requirements for working in data entry and data capture vary depending on the client and the nature of the job. In general, however, fast typing skills and a high level of concentration are an advantage. Familiarity with various data processing programs and databases is also important.

One way to get involved in this field is to look for online jobs or work with companies that specialize in this type of service. There are also platforms that connect freelancers with companies that need data entry services.

In summary, Data Entry and Data Entry are important activities that are needed in many companies. It is an option for people who have good writing skills, high concentration level and would like to work in the field of data processing.

Useful web links to online platforms that list job openings in Data Entry and Data Capture:

- Upwork – https://www.upwork.com

- Freelancer – https://www.freelancer.com

- Clickworker – https://www.clickworker.com

- Microworkers – https://www.microworkers.com

- Amazon Mechanical Turk – https://www.mturk.com

There are also some specialized platforms that focus on data collection and analysis. We have compiled a small selection for you here:

- CrowdFlower – https://www.crowdflower.com

- Tableau – https://www.tableau.com

- Splunk – https://www.splunk.com

- Qlik View – https://www.qlik.com

- RapidWorkers – https://rapidworkers.com

- Haddop – https://hadoop.apache.org

However, it is important to be cautious when working with these platforms and ensure that the work is fairly compensated and that there is no data misuse or fraud.

16. Transcription and audio text creation

Transcription and audio text creation is another option for working online. It refers to the conversion of audio or video files into text documents. This work is suitable for people with good listening skills and fast writing speed.

Transcription work can be done for a variety of clients including corporations, research institutions, media companies, educational institutions, and many others. Transcriptions can come from interviews, meetings, conferences, dictations, podcasts, lectures, and many other types of audio or video recordings.

There are two types of transcription tasks, verbatim and non-verbatim. Verbatim transcriptions capture all the words and utterances spoken in the audio recording, including background noise, laughter and pauses. Non-verbatim transcriptions include only the most important information spoken in the audio recording.

Transcription typically requires a computer, a headset, and transcription software. There are many free and paid transcription tools that can be used to make the job easier. Tasks are usually paid per minute of audio (PMA) or per hour of work (PHA).

Compensation is usually based on the difficulty of the audio material and the volume of the transcription. In addition to transcription, online audio copywriters can also provide services such as subtitling, translation, and audio translation.

For people who enjoy working alone and are passionate about audio and voice recording, transcription and audio copywriting may be a good fit. Good articulation, fast typing, and excellent spelling and grammar are essential for this work.

It is important to note that this work requires time and patience, as it is often necessary to delve into the audio material and make many corrections in order to produce a detailed text.

Useful web links to online platforms offering transcription and audio text creation services:

- Rev – https://www.rev.com

- TranscribeMe – https://www.transcribeme.com

- Scribie – https://scribie.com

- GoTranscript – https://gotranscript.com

- Speechpad – https://www.speechpad.com

There are many other platforms that offer similar services. However, it is important to carefully consider which platform best suits your needs.

17. Technical support and helpdesk

Technical support and help desk are tasks that require expertise and technical knowledge to assist customers with technical problems and provide solutions. Support may be provided by phone, e-mail, or remote access to the customer's computer.

A help desk employee must be able to answer technical questions from customers and guide them through possible solutions. This can include problems with hardware, software, or network connectivity. It is also important to have excellent interpersonal skills. This ensures that the customer is well taken care of at every stage of the support process.

Tech support and help desk work can be a great way to work from home, as many companies offer remote work and flexible hours. Skills and qualifications required can vary depending on the employer. However, experience in the IT or technical support industry is often essential.

A technical support or help desk professional may also work as a consultant, helping companies improve their IT systems and processes. This field may also involve creating training and educational materials to help users improve their technical skills.

In summary, technical support and help desk is a great way to assist customers with technical issues and help companies optimize their IT systems.

Useful web links that provide information and resources on technical support and help desk:

- HDI – https://www.thinkhdi.com

- Freshdesk – https://freshdesk.com/helpdesk-software

- G2 Crowd – https://www.g2crowd.com/categories/help-desk

- Capterra – https://www.capterra.com/help-desk-software

- Zendesk – https://www.zendesk.com/resources/help-desk-software

- Spiceworks – https://www.spiceworks.com/free-help-desk-software

- ITIL – https://www.axelos.com/certifications/itil-service-management

18. Online training and e-learning

Online training and e-learning is a great way to transfer knowledge and skills online. More and more people are taking advantage of this type of training to advance their careers, learn new skills, or simply continue their education for personal use.

Online training can come in a variety of formats. These include video lessons, live webinars, interactive courses, and more. Courses can be free or paid, depending on the provider and content.

Online training is available in many areas, including languages, programming, digital marketing, design, cooking, fitness, and many others. There are numerous platforms where you can find such courses, and many of them offer certificates or degrees to increase the value to the participant.

Flexibility and the ability to access courses anytime, anywhere are the benefits of online training and e-learning. They are also often less expensive than traditional training formats and offer the ability to focus on specific topics.

For companies, e-learning platforms also offer the opportunity to train employees and ensure that they are always up to date.

Useful web links about online training and e-learning:

- **Udemy** – https://www.udemy.com
  Udemy is an online learning platform with courses on various topics and skills. The courses are created and offered by experts.

- **Coursera** – https://www.coursera.org
  Coursera is an online platform that offers courses from renowned universities and companies around the world.

- **edX** – https://www.edx.org
  edX is a free online platform that offers courses from top universities around the world.

- **Skillshare** – https://www.skillshare.com
  Skillshare is an online platform for creative courses, including design, photography, illustration and more.

- **Khan Academy** – https://de.khanacademy.org
  Khan Academy is a free online platform for students of all ages, offering courses on various topics and sub-jects.

- **LinkedIn Learning** –
  https://www.linkedin.com/learning
  LinkedIn is an online learning platform from LinkedIn that offers courses on a variety of topics, including business, technology, and creativity.

- **OpenLearn** – https://www.open.edu/openlearn
  OpenLearn is a free online learning platform from the
  Open University that offers courses and resources on
  a variety of topics.

- **Codecademy** – https://www.codecademy.com
  Codecademy is an online coding skills development
  platform that offers courses on various programming
  languages.

- **FutureLearn** – https://www.futurelearn.com
  FutureLearn is an online learning platform that offers
  courses on various topics from top universities and
  companies.

- **Teachable** – https://teachable.com
  Teachable is an online platform that allows anyone to
  create and sell courses. The platform offers tools and
  resources to create and manage courses.

19. Game testing and evaluation

One way to make money online is to test and review games. Game testing is the process of checking the content, features, graphics, and other aspects of video games to make sure that they run smoothly and provide a fun and entertaining experience. This is an important step in game development, as bugs and errors need to be discovered before the game is released.

There are several types of games that can be tested, including console, PC, and mobile games. To ensure that they test all aspects of the game, testers are usually given a guide or checklist to follow. The results are then shared with the developer or publisher to fix problems and improve the gaming experience.

As a game tester, you can either be hired directly by the developer or you can be hired through a specialized testing company. Pay can vary depending on the company and the type of work, but is generally between 10 and 20 Euros per hour. Some companies also offer bonuses or other perks such as free games or hardware.

In addition to testing games, you can also earn money by reviewing games. In this case, you'll be asked to give your opinion about a game by playing it and writing a review. These ratings are used by game developers and publishers to get feedback from players and improve the game experience.

Overall, video game testing and rating is a fun activity to make money online, especially for those who have a passion for video games. It requires patience, attention to details and the ability to formulate feedback constructively.

Useful web links about game testing and evaluation:

- **Testbirds** – https://www.testbirds.com/de
  Testbirds is a company that offers crowdsourced testing services and is always looking for new testers. Here you can apply to be a tester and work on games and other software products.

- **Glassdoor** – https://www.glassdoor.de
  Glassdoor is a website where employees can anonymously share salary information and employer reviews. On the site you can find information about salaries of game testers in different companies.

- **Gamestar** – https://www.gamestar.de
  On Gamestar you can find a detailed description of the job profile of a game tester. The page provides insights into the daily work and the requirements of the job.

- **Spieletester.de** – https://www.spieletester.de
  Spieletester.de is a platform where players can test games and give their reviews. Here you can register as a tester and work on different games.

- **Gamasutra** – https://jobs.gamedeveloper.com
  Gamasutra is a website focused on news and career opportunities in the games industry. Here you can find a list of job opportunities in quality assurance and game testing.

20. Customer service and support

The ability to provide customer service and support is critical for many businesses to provide the best possible service and support to their customers. With the growing number of online customers, the need for fast and effective customer support has become essential for businesses.

Online customer service and support involves a variety of tasks, including answering customer inquiries via email, chat, or phone; handling orders and complaints; performing technical support tasks; and providing training and tutorials to customers. Good customer service can build customer trust and loyalty, which can lead to business growth and success.

Working in customer service and support typically requires a strong customer focus, quick thinking, good communication skills, the ability to work in a team, and a positive attitude. Experience using customer relationship management (CRM) systems and other support tools may also be an advantage.

There are several ways to work in online customer service and support. For example, you can work for a company as a customer service representative or work independently as a virtual assistant for various clients. Starting your own online support company is another way to work in this field.

Overall, working in customer service and support provides good options to work from home while improving customer service and satisfaction.

Useful web links on the subject of customer service and support are:

- **Zendesk** – https://www.zendesk.com
  A leading customer interaction and support platform that provides tools for ticketing, chat, messaging and self-service options.

- **Freshdesk** – https://freshdesk.com
  An all-in-one customer support software that offers features such as ticketing, chat, messaging, telephony and social media integration.

- **HubSpot Service Hub** – https://www.hubspot.de
  A customer service platform that provides ticketing and messaging capabilities, chatbots, customer feedback tools, and reporting capabilities.

- **Zoho Desk** – https://www.zoho.com/desk
  A cloud-based customer service platform that offers features such as ticketing, chat, messaging, telephony and social media integration.

- **Intercom** – https://www.intercom.com
  An all-in-one customer engagement and communication platform that offers features such as messaging, live chat, customer feedback tools, and automation capabilities.

- **Help Scout** – https://www.helpscout.com
  A customer support platform that provides email, chat, messaging, phone support, and automation capabilities.

- **Groove** – https://www.groovehq.com
  An easy-to-use customer support software with features like ticketing, chat, messaging and customer feedback tools.

- **Kayako** – https://www.kayako.com
  A customer service platform that offers features such as ticketing, chat, messaging, and social media integration, as well as automated workflows and reporting capabilities.

- **LiveAgent** – https://www.liveagent.de
  An all-in-one customer support platform with features such as ticketing, chat, messaging, telephony, social media integration and automation capabilities.

V. Practical tips for successful work from home

How to stay productive

When you work from home, it's often difficult to stay productive. Here are some tips that can help you stay focused and productive.

1. **Set up a workstation**

    A fixed workspace helps keep you mentally focused on your work. A tidy and organized workplace promotes productivity.

2. **Set priorities**

    Setting priorities and creating a daily schedule can help you focus on the most important tasks and avoid distractions.

3. **Avoid distractions**

    Distractions like social media, watching TV, or surfing the web can cause you to lose focus quickly. Try to minimize these distractions by not answering private messages or calls during work hours.

4. **Take breaks**

    Taking regular breaks can help maintain productivity and reduce stress. A short break every few hours can help refresh your body and mind.

5. **Keep routines**

    A set routine helps keep you focused on work and separate your work life from your personal life.

6. **Avoid multitasking**

    Multitasking can often leave you unable to focus on one thing, making you more productive when you focus on one task at a time.

7. **Reward yourself**

    Setting yourself small rewards can help keep you motivated and more productive. A fresh cup of coffee with a piece of chocolate can work wonders.

It is important to note that everyone is different and needs to try different techniques to find what works best for them.

How to organize

Effective organization is critical to successful working from home. Here are some tips on how best to get organized.

1. **Create a work plan**
    Determine what tasks you need to complete and when you will complete them. A well-planned work schedule can help you focus on your work and use your time wisely.

2. **Use a to-do list**
    Write down all the tasks that need to be done on a list and prioritize them by urgency. A to-do list can help you stay focused and make sure you don't forget any important tasks.

3. **Create a workspace**
    A tidy and organized workspace can help you focus on your work and be more productive.

4. **Avoid distractions**
    Make sure you have no distractions during your work hours. Turn off your phone and close all unnecessary browser windows and applications on your computer.

5. **Improve the way you work**
    It is important to continuously improve and optimize the way you work. One way, for example, is to regularly seek feedback from supervisors or colleagues to identify and implement potential improvements. Developing new skills and techniques can also help optimize work.

6. **Set clear goals**

Define clear goals for your work and track your progress regularly. This way you can motivate yourself and increase your productivity.

7. **Use time management tools**

There are many time management tools that can help organize and schedule tasks and projects. Some common tools include to-do lists, calendar apps, and project management tools. These can help keep track of tasks and deadlines and streamline work.

8. **Stay motivated**

Motivation is an important factor in staying productive and optimizing your work. It can be helpful to set clear goals and follow through to increase your sense of accomplishment. Creating rewards for reaching milestones can also help maintain motivation.

Good organization can help you be more productive and get more done. Try different strategies and find out which ones work best for you.

How to stay healthy and fit

When you work from home, it can often be hard to get enough exercise and eat healthy. The following recommendations can help you stay healthy and fit.

1. **Create a productive work environment**

   One of the greatest benefits of working from home is the ability to create your own work environment. It's important to create an area that's free of distractions and where you can focus. A well-lit, spacious workspace with a comfortable seating position can help you be more productive and efficient.

2. **Get up every few hours**

   Get up regularly to walk a few steps or do some simple stretches. This promotes blood circulation and helps with stiffness and pain.

3. **Keep plenty of healthy snacks on hand**

   Healthy snacks, such as nuts, fruits or vegetables, can keep blood sugar levels stable and provide energy without taxing the body.

4. **Make sure you have a balanced diet**

   Make sure you have a balanced diet and drink enough water. Avoid eating junk food all day or drinking too much coffee and alcohol.

5. **Schedule regular breaks**

   Take regular short breaks to relax or do some yoga or breathing exercises. This can help relieve stress and maintain focus.

6. **Get enough sleep**

    Get enough sleep to make sure you have enough energy and focus to get through the day.

7. **Exercise regularly**

    Try to incorporate sports or exercise into your daily routine on a regular basis, such as a short jog, yoga or strength training. It can help keep the body fit and strengthen the immune system.

VI. Conclusion and Outlook

Summary of key findings

We have now presented you with 20 concrete ways to make money from home in our guide. We have covered a variety of areas, including online surveys, blogging, social media management, online teaching, and much more. Each offers a unique opportunity to work from home and earn a steady, secure income.

Key findings in the overview:

1. There are a variety of ways to work from home and earn money.

2. It takes time, patience and commitment to be successful.

3. It is important to find a niche and focus on a specific area of expertise.

4. Effective self-organization, time management and productivity are critical to success.

5. It is important to continuously learn and develop in order to remain competitive.

6. A positive attitude and a good work-life balance are important for long-term success.

7. ChatGPT artificial intelligence can provide us with excellent support in many areas, making it easier than ever to make money online.

So overall, working from home offers many benefits, but it also requires discipline and commitment. Technology has enabled us to work flexibly and achieve a better work-life balance. However, we should be aware that there are also challenges, such as isolation and distractions. It's important to have realistic expectations and work hard to succeed.

Future prospects for home work

The future of working from home in a home office is more promising today than ever before. With the increasing digitalization and expansion of the Internet, there will be even more opportunities to work from home in the future. The world of work will continue to change significantly in the coming years, and working from home will play an increasingly important role.

The fact that working from home can be successfully implemented in many industries and companies has been demonstrated by the Corona pandemic. More and more companies are recognizing the benefits of working from home, such as saving on space costs or the ability to find talented employees in other parts of the world.

The combination of artificial intelligence (AI) and working from home is another forward-looking development. More and more tasks can be automated by AI systems, making working from home even more efficient. We believe that ChatGPT will play an important role in our daily work. It can help us achieve our goals, inspire us and give us new ideas. It can help us to be more productive while freeing up time for the important things in life.

ChatGPT can be a real blessing in an increasingly hectic world where we have more and more responsibilities. It can help us simplify our lives and find a healthy work-life balance.

The rapid development of technology and the ever-changing demands of the world of work will shape the future of working from home. It is likely that more and more people will be working from home in their own Home Office 3.0 and that the way we work will change significantly in the future.

www.ingramcontent.com/pod-product-compliance
Lightning Source LLC
Chambersburg PA
CBHW061345140726
47997CB00003B/1056